CONTENTS

5	Pigeon grounded
6	Continuum
8	'Home thoughts from abroad'
10	Cyberspace nights
12	Isolation
15	First and last moments
18	'It's art, but is it clever?'
19	'Beauty is in the eye'
20	Tattyphilia
21	Fashion for beauty
22	Haiku
23	Portmanteau
24	Panther in a tree
25	Lottery gluttony (propitiation)
26	Limericks
27	Elitism 1990s
27	Saint Valentine
28	Spring, a resurrection
29	Still waters shiver
30	The other side of violet
31	Enwombed
32	Footsteps sound on the stair
33	Death
34	Country living (plus ça change)
38	My dreams are strangers
41	Timeless
43	Aunt Violet
44	Mother love
45	The fleeting hours
47	Witchcraft
49	Words
50	Varmints
51	The room grows cold
54	Airborne on springs
56	Autumn, a chance to sleep
58	Ladies with cellos
60	Fishing for tiddlers
63	'The bliss of solitude'

PIGEON GROUNDED

Acorns were plentiful under the branches
Pigeons went scratching among the dead leaves
Stuffing their crops till their gizzards protruded
And breasts were swelled out like kitchen tureens

Twigs snapping and cracking meant man was approaching
Heads raised in alarm they were suddenly chill
Whirring and flapping, wings sprang into action -
Except for one pigeon whose legs stayed stock-still

Lift-off defeated by overload intake
Fear-bulging eyes watched those vanishing clowns -
Came the sharp crack of a two-barrelled shot-gun
Bodies came crashing and plummeting down

As he gazed upwards, the pale blue of heaven
Was crossed by a beaky-nosed monster in white
Roaring away in complacent perfection
Flat-bellied, untroubled by gluttony's plight

Cowering uncomfortable, feeling dyspeptic,
Wanting to crap but not daring to move
He thought of high gliders, balloons, bats and insects,
Of flights of ideas, how men fly to the moon

He pondered the problems of aerodynamics
Of buoyancy, gravity, air and the wind
Oscillation and radar and uplift and braking -
And knew these were futile until he had thinned

He thought of the fishes that swim in the ocean
For swimming is flight not supported by air
Graceful, curvaceous, free-soaring or diving
Unhampered by stomachs weighed down by their fare

Then he thought of the foxes the owls and the badgers
Scouring the woods for some succulent pie
Lured by the plumpness and warmth of his body -
He shot out the husks and shot up in the sky.

CONTINUUM

They say the universe is all within ourselves -
Why then in *me* ! for there is no one else
The cats, the guns, the oceans, bombs and trees,
Outside me cease to be

A host of angels balance on a pin
Transform themselves into an evil djinn
Face pressed to mine volcanic mouth a-grin
He whirls away wrapped sheets in dervish spin

They say there are no angels, pins or djinns
I say there are no theys - I always win
A blackbird's bright-eyed head lets out a sigh
Its yellow beak holds up the pastry of a rabbit pie

They say the world outside sends messages
Along the pathways of my sensing nerves
A loaf of bread they see and I see too
A hearty smack would tell you who is who

How else would I feel shock and pain and grief
Regret, anxiety and disbelief?
If all the people in the world agree
It's simple! They're not separate, they're in me

It's dark outside I draw the curtains tight
Turn out the cupboards switching on the light
My memory hops across the stepping stones
Of stream of consciousness, no parking zones

Don't look behind the bushes you might find
A Michelangelo or Hokusai
Cleaned paintings rimed patina scoured away
Dark corners' mysteries made brash by day.

They say we'll check it by experiment
By scientific tests not temperament -
Emotions blocked appear like traffic cones
Old paths diverted into ways unknown

Now trepidation straps me cruelly down
My shrieking voice a whisper *I shall drown*
Soft duvets suffocate my nostrils' air
Wheels skid down icy roads towards despair

Moon has two sides and I would choose the dark
Wander down quiet lanes, be still, and hear dogs bark
A seagull calling as it skims the bars
Wild thoughts exploding into shooting stars

If what is in is fed by what is out
And what is out
Projected from within
The boundary between is very thin
A sensate interface may or may not
Keep them in place.

'HOME THOUGHTS FROM ABROAD'
(BROWNING)

I travel much I cannot tell
Where I shall wake at morning light
Up in the air or down a well
On windswept mountain's frosty height
Or rock-strewn deserts scorching bright

I freeze, I burn, I soar, I sink
It's all the same to me and mine
Let there be comfort, food and drink
The earth beneath, the stars that shine
The pleasures of a concubine

My home is held within my heart
For that is where my childhood lies
The timelessness of tribal art
My origins epitomise
My place of birth between two thighs

Remembered house, remembered pains,
Remembered joys, fragmented days
The rain-filled gutters, gurgling drains
A hornet's nest, the fireside's blaze
Long feathered grass and cow's soft gaze

Such trivia are my true home
Unique to me by no one shared
Essentially I am alone
No one can *feel* how much I cared
No words convey emotions bared

A country though - a piece of land
Inviolate, save crumbling cliffs
And silted harbours, shifting sand
With woods and pastures, monoliths
And trains defaced by hieroglyphs

All cities have their counterpart
In shopping malls and petrol fumes
Tall buildings tearing clouds apart
With streets like canyons winding through
And skylined teeth too worn to chew

A nomad of the soul am I
Rejecting land, discarding nest
The memories my brain supplies
I suck for solace seeking rest
My home is still my mother's breast.

Lengthening shadows are crossing the moon
Code names are surfing the cyberspace boom
Under the skin of the child's angel head
Hides the white skull of the forthcoming dead

Atoms are drifting spaced out in the dark
Compacted in solids, in gases more stark
Phantom miasma, we float on the crust
Illusion, reality, which can we trust?

Nothing is permanent, all can be changed
Transmuted, refuted, computed, arranged
Identity lost in the shuffling of genes
Nature gives way to our engineered schemes

Life is a welter of DNA spirals
Dancing through time till death forces retirals
Rotating, mutating through billions of years
Revolving, evolving impermanent spheres

Telescopes pick up the spooks of the past
Beamed out towards us by planets and stars
X-rays and infra-red, UV and cosmic
Strike through our delicate flesh and enrot it

Unfelt and untasted, unheard and unseen
Nuclear fingers cause damage obscene.
Mystics and mediums process the vibes
Make recent departees corporealize

Magical miracles stream from the gods
Quanta are charged to manipulate mobs
In formatting atoms the limits are blurred
Disbelief is suspended and faith disinterred

What isn't predictable cannot be true
Inscrutable science has mixed points of view
Strobes interfere with our brain-scan vibrata
Air waves can ruin our hearing pro rata

Computers take messages out of our heads
Encode them as binary bytes it is said
Then modems convey them as frequency sections
By wires to their partners, so making connections

Browsing the Web like a purposeful spider
Led by the Internet's Service Provider
Following Protocol's laid-down inflections
Whizzing via satellites' linked-up selections -

In cycles per second, vibrating to measure
Suburbia gossips are sharing their treasure
Cyberspace Netiquette faithfully hammed
Bots* are the goodies while Spams* should be banned

Invisible worlds gather round us like ghosts
As we gorge our emotions on aerial soaps
Hauntingly linger, electro-magnetic
Making our brief lives seem rather pathetic
Our atom-bound bodies no more than cosmetic
Our very existence in space theoretic
Activities purposeless wasted frenetic
And then we're expected to be sympathetic

Bits of the universe ageless, eternal
Our limited vision states we are supernal
Restless and lonely as atomless sprites
We're just an extension of cyberspace nights.

**Spam: a reference to the World War 2 canned meat loaf, rubbish-rated junk food, hence a clogging of the computer with junk mail.*

**Bot: abbreviation for Robot - an automated computer program that can wipe out Spams.*

ISOLATION

A barrier separates me from the world outside
Impenetrable shield that will not yield
A window through which none can see
Except me

Wraiths come and go, drifting before my eyes, remote
As dreams, a shadow play, untouched, untouchable
Empty as plundered husks, discarded shells
Senseless as aimless flitting fish entanked

They zoom up close, spy me with plundering eyes,
See nothing but a two-way mirror shafting back
The bright reflections of their own desires -
Myself a plaster mannequin, immobile dummy

I cower within, a crafty feral cur,
Watching with stealth these aliens, enemies,
Their eyes agog, seeking to pierce my shell,
Out-suck my soul, ingrafting me

Hot-drenched with fear I scream I turn and twist
And no one hears.
The mask implacable shuts in the sound,
Seems calm, while rocks of agonized despair
Crush me beneath them. Torn between wanting
And not wanting help
I cannot speak.

They knock upon my shell, goading response, as boys
Thumping for endless hours a ball
Upon a stranger's wall
Wait for the wide-flung door, the angry shout
The gleeful triumph of their provocation

Dumb and remote, a prisoner of my own security
Trapped like Houdini in his failed escape
The panic mounting to a surging roar
I cannot trust

A closed portcullis lies across my throat
The torment of frustration cannot shift
The leaden weight that anchors down my tongue
Communication is too perilous

I feel myself a fledgling bird, grotesque,
Naked and vulnerable,
Torn in a thousand blundering parts
That rush colliding with the speed of light
And cannot join.
Peck with divided will the inner shell,
And leave no mark.

Even when they come close - *Don't touch!*
I shall disintegrate, shrivel and split apart! -
They are unreal.
I want to be like them, to move at ease
To smile, to laugh, and not forever weep . . .
What *are* they?

Give me a knife, let me drag out their hearts
Their brains their guts their feelings
Take them to pieces like a watch
Unpower the battery, break the tight-wound spring
I need to know!

They tease me, try to prise away my shell, dismember me
Consume me like a soft defenceless crab
Quick! I must hide, pretend a marble effigy -
Rather a living corpse sealed in a lead-lined coffin.
I cannot move

If I could only tell the loneliness,
The agony of isolation, the despair.
Their hatred freezes me - *my* hatred?

And all the time within the fury builds
Feelings untempered by communication
Pain undiluted by a tide of anger
So strong so powerful I'm consumed with frenzy -
As if, breaking a window into gaping splinters
The inrushed air boils to a blazing furnace
I must burst forth, escape . . .

Visions of misery, breaking splintered limbs
The jagged bones pierced through the bloody flesh
Terrors of space, of death, damp mouldering walls,
Of houses falling, earth beneath my feet
Dropping away

Hug back the shell,
Wrap it around me -
And choke within the turmoil of my own emotions?
Prison myself in this confined restraint
Against invasion from some alien world
Aeons away across the universe
In other planets?

The grisly seesaw sways vertiginous:
Violence or death.

Fasten a chain around my neck and lead me out
Teach me to speak to trust not care too much,
To live upon the surface dancing light
The furious wolves of passion shut below
Secure from ravaging my tender ego

But what if they leap forth, autistic Frankensteins,
Towering like gods above the common herd
Conquering the world with their omnipotence
Glorious, destructive, and in full control
Ah then - and then -

If that could only last
And I could kill all those who tortured me,
And those who might
Then I would know a unity so sweet
A peace so dear, revenge so comforting -
My enemies destroyed, *then I could live!*

FIRST AND LAST MOMENTS

When was I *I?*
Was it in that first millisecond
of conjunction
when fastest racing sperm invaded egg
merging to lose itself
into a greater whole
robotically computerised by acids?

Was it when brain and nerves
grew in my still-bent head
neck slashed with gills
bathed in warm fluid where I lay at ease
fed without effort, cushioned from all shock
reclining hedonist yet
anchored by a cord
a mere appendix of another's body?

Was it when cruel contractions thrust my skull
out through the bony arch of Eden's garden
evicted from that paradise of darkness
onto earth from water,
surrounded by a dry and alien gas
pervasive, frightening . . .
But, beyond control,
my chest leapt heaving outwards
baring my lungs' vast labyrinth of naked tubes
to air's exultant entry -
Then repelled it
in one vast yell of angonising protest.

Then was I *I,* for planets on their journeys
clicked on their stopwatch at my birth's divorce
formatting daily destiny in signs and numbers
entering the software of my lifetime's course.

Now I was separate though my mother's caring
essayed to recreate the pampering womb
wrapped warmly, head supported, sleeping softly
the gushing nipple ready to consume.

Yet still the world, my world, remained inside me
a narcissistic game of make-believe
with I omnipotent, controlling player
the rest just shadows that might hurt or please.

This I am *I* engendered desolation
an *I* no one can ever fully know
a landscape only seen through omens, shadows,
wolves baying at the moon, the frozen snow.

And isolation grew with my awareness
the shadows were not under my control
the consciousness that there were others round me
each one an I, each one a separate whole.

Deprived of instinct's automatic actions -
its force direct emotion, bold and free -
cursed with an ego-knowledge and with reason
how could I interact with others yet stay me?

Each from his inner prison venturing outwards,
like sniffer dogs we go from clue to clue,
observe, interpret, calculate, make judgments
on others aims, if friendly or untrue.

Only in love, in race perpetuation
our egos willingly reject their rights
will suffer, starve, be maimed to save their offspring
beyond all reason seek self-sacrifice.

And at some point in time to be determined
my *I* will find itself at death's wide door
its consciousness will fall into a stupor
its brain dysfunction, reason, thought withdraw.

My body will be food for necrophages
consuming flesh that once was ego's pride
converting me to beneficial vapours
that plants incorporate to stay alive.

My complex parts disintegrate to liquids
seep down into the soil dissolved by rain
dispersing far and wide my human richness
- particulate and unidentified.

So, when will the *I* of me be *I* no longer?
Will it be when
In the reverse of that first fusion
I become de-fused
disintegrated and no longer one?

Or when nerves and brain
finally lack an interface of skin
to sense the world,
a team of muscles
to condition impulse,
a shape's parameters
to keep me whole -
now all is derelict?

Where will I lodge
that I that knows I'm *I*
unique and separate from other I's?
Will that great conscious *I* also disperse
windborne, ten thousand fluffy willow seeds
hovering lightly
floating on the breeze
free of a flesh encasement,
gladly free of fear,
ambition, thought, constraint, desire?
Or be recaptured, whole or in its parts
juggled, recycled, jigsaw-like assembled
into another *I* to which I'm nothing
a continuity of substance, not of self?
If this is so,
Then I shall never know.
The planets have moved on
I am the past
their stop-watch set for others
and my file deleted.

'IT'S ART BUT IS IT CLEVER?'

(THOUGHTS ON 1990s ART)
(KIPLING REVERSED)

I took a sentence from a reference book
And snipped it into bite-sized pieces
Arranged in lines of irregular length
So I made poetry out of prose.
I took a box of bricks
Plagiarising a child's toy in the windows of Mothercare
And sold it to a credulous art gallery
For a fortune.

In their manual act of arranging the bricks
Curators felt they had discovered some basic truth
About the universe
That no one before them had ever had the wit to perceive -
Like the Emperor in his non-clothes
Parading naked through the streets.
Sure, that was art, or artfulness
On the part of the non-weaving non-sewing tailors
Conning the man's vanity till he never could admit
He saw nothing.

Why not (never ask why) display a sleeping girl
In a vitrine
Like a drunk snoring on the grass in the park
In full view, his hand inside his unflyed trousers -
Now there's genius.

Make art reversible
The tail must wag the dog, for the horse is drawn by the cart,
As Kipling said. Go further,
Put the poem lines end to end
Take out the stops and commas, the hard returns
And you are back where you started.
Stow the bricks away in their box,
Let the girl step out of her glass showcase,
Take down the breakfast dish from the wall -
But remember it was not the cook but the person who
Hung up the plate
That was the artist.

Once art was perfectionist, seeking to communicate
With tireless perseveration
Some interpretation of reality
That was life-enhancing - no money in *that!*

Better to fling pots of clashing colours
Over the floor, roll in them like a dog in dung
And in a flash you have a masterpiece
Re-define art, and even garbage is art
Or arty anyway
Flip it top to bottom, inside out,
An android piddling patterns in the dust - what else?
But clever? Synthetic judgments of subjective art?
What can I say.

'BEAUTY IS IN THE EYE'
(MARGARET WOLFE HUNGERFORD)

Beauty is in the eye, cast out the mote
If you would keep your sanity afloat
The world is ugly, *vide* the current soaps
Reality's destruction - exit hopes

A harmony of form, a cool precision
Expressed in words - an object of derision
Though once the highest of artistic vision
Now poetry and life are in collision

How else adapt this concept of aesthetics
Drag it to earth, materialise its ethics?
Beauty is truth? Tell that to vain cosmetics
A joy for ever? Pass me the emetics.

We, surface living, have no wish to feel
Beauty disturbs the depths we would conceal.

TATTYPHILIA

(REFLECTIONS ON AN EXHIBITION. IS ART SIMPLY THE ORDINARY TAKEN OUT OF CONTEXT?)

Spot lights strike between the wires
of animal cages
thin shadow lines project upon the walls
paintings by Mondrian.
But the fidgeting bodies of once lively occupants
are absent
nothing moves
in this predictable geometric world.

Here in a darkened corner, on a screen
a video follows a fibre-optic camera
crawling along a muscular vagine
edging voyeuristically towards the cervix -
inspiring a way-out hostess to bore her guests
with moving pictures of her gut endoscopy
a ramble through a cornfield of pink fingers
that wave autonomically at the passing light.

Bisected cow and calf, semi-fresh
from the abbatoire, chopped down their long axes
into more or less symmetrical
dexter and sinister portions
copies of class-room biology models
demonstrating offal-filled bodies.
In life their pulsating secrets glistened
moss-green, canary yellow, crimson rose,
now dulled to tempera, dowsed in formaldehyde.
This did not need an artist
only a slaughter-house operative with a cleaver
a saw, fixatives and a big container.

Unremarkable objects lifted out of context
artistic as chamber pots on a church steeple,
juxtaposed in a void-of-life environment
for browsing incognoscenti who, baffled but excited,
prattle *How beautiful!,* congratulate the Director
on his progressive originality.
Truth was he, Friend-dependent and
starved of genuine artefacts,
had to make do with fakes.

FASHION FOR BEAUTY

Though fashions strive to woo the fickle marts
And claw their way to top the season's charts
No fashion's permanent by definition
For new is always good, and old perdition.

Unchanging beauty stands above such ploys
The pop-scene fad's no more than soft-sell toys
Inflating ego-puffs of wealth and passion
Inconstancy's the constant mark of fashion.

The starch-cruel ruffs, cosmetic surgeons' dream,
Cheeks arsenic white with spots of crimson cream,
Hips sawdust-padded, spread by farthingales
Or lipo-sucked to make them lean as males',
Bust-flatteners, whalebones stays, and platform shoes
Lace-decorated men and dugs like ewes
All peaks of beauty while the fashion lasts
Abyss of ugliness when it has passed -
Such anti-beauty's nothing more than lies
Beauty abused to capture envious eyes.

Commercial fashions are a taste acquired
Only by contrast can they seem desired
True beauty's changeless, timeless as the sun
It bonds us with the object, makes us one
No restless striving moneyed palms to grease
Instead a sense of unity and peace.

A fallen carpet of rose-petalled flowers
The glinting light on slanting April showers
Cadence of music, dancers light as air
A life-enhancing harmony, so rare
A friendly greeting as of outstretched hands
Beauty I know you, feel not understand.

HAIKU

Tears drop from his eyes
A dewdrop clings to his nose
Earth and sky weep pain

Licking the wet fur
Cat fondles the dying mouse
Purring sinks his teeth

The fox faces death
Loneliness closes its eyes
One against too many.

The clouds hang heavy
Grains of snow powder the wind
Frozen confetti.

Across the shiny tiles
Sole slaps against sole
Walking reflections.

The girl said *Quack!*
Yellow ducklings run to her
She is their mother.

Lonely woodlouse
Trapped in a stainless steel sink
Greets its reflection.

Hermaphrodite worm
No Lonely Hearts, no Blind Dates
Itself sufficient.

The breeze stirs
Kaleidoscope of shadows
Under green branches.

The crysalis unzips
Mayfly stretches its wings
Twelve hours to die.

PORTMANTEAU

I carry my body like a portmanteau
It holds all my necessities
And travels with me
Wherever I go
Sometimes on a train
I wish I could put it on the luggage rack
And leave it there.

Sometimes it seems
As though it's not a separate item at all
But the skin of an enemy
And that, like the Aztecs I have climbed inside
Pulling it over me
To neutralize its hatred -

Reminds me of that tale,
How a large dog was flayed
And its skin stitched over a tiny dog
Swaddled in kilos of immensely valuable lace
To be sent stumbling across the frontier
Into France, and there undressed
Of its encumbrances.

When my portmanteau was new
It gave me pleasure to display it
I looked after it well
And admired its beauty
It's old now, dried in the sun
Scuffed at the corners
Tagged with luggage labels
It seems heavy and awkward to carry
Sometimes I'm almost too tired to pick it up.

One day it will rot and fall apart,
I shall put it down
A sloughed-off casing,
I shall stretch myself
And swish away lighter than air
To join the other passengers
Who have also lost their portmanteaux
And do not want them back.

PANTHER IN A TREE

A beer can windblown along the cobbled street
Clatters and stops.
Above the rain-soaked shoes
The drunk bends down,
Lids droop on wine-fazed eyes
Hands like stiff twigs
Brush across the stones,
Near-blindly lift the water-dripping can
To feel-dry lips.
Droplets fall on his skin
He tilts his head
Sees in the bare tree branches overhead
Cold citron eyes in jet-black panther face
Cruel teeth white-gleamed
Look out! he shouts
His voice reverberates
Throughout the night-hushed square
Look out!
Sleek with disdain
The panther glides,
Its paw - sledgehammer spiked with nails -
Strikes down a child, a man, a dog, a multitude
Blood spurts in crimson fountains
Arms, hands and feet fly through the air
He stands, swaying
Harsh voice
Echoes from far-off walls
It's killing everyone!
Don't you bloody care?
Everyone is dead! is dead! is dead!
Don't you ever bloody listen?
He pounds the air
Hurrying footsteps pause, throat giggles,
Steps pass on
He tries to sit
Misses
Hits the ground
It hurts
He lies there
And suddenly he weeps.

LOTTERY GLUTTONY
(PROPITIATION)

If I should win I'd plant a grove of trees
Where nuns could walk
I'd rid the world of nuclear unease
Teach pets to talk
I'd open up the vistas to the sun
Make all men one
I'd cleanse the air and wipe the smog away
Converse with angels on the Milky Way.

I'd find a cure for suicidal cells
Dig useful wells
I'd make the world revolve around my whims
Mend broken limbs
I'd have the roof repaired, walls underpinned
Save those who sinned . . .
I'll throw the dice when all the cards are dealt
And Chance's icy heart must surely melt.

I'd buy a steak for everyone who's poor -
They'd ask for more
I'd clip the naughty politicians' wings
Let boys be kings
For what is money if we cannot choose
To win or lose . . .
Too late too late to change my wishful dreams
Now let the god appear from the machines.

My fate is sealed. Are promises enough
To prove I'm worthy of the lucky touch?
Through life our lack of fortune we berail
Let chance take over where our egos fail.
Dear god of Chance I pray you on my knees
Just tell me please oh please, how I *can* please.

A pop-art collector of Mayfair
Went searching for talent in Times Square
    It thrilled him to find
    Random paint strokes unsigned
By a cat sharpening claws on an armchair.
(Ref: picture-painting cats in California)

A pretty web-browser of Cheam
Complained I am stuck to the screen
    The Internet spider
    Has hypnotised Lisa
And now I'm the site of its dreams.

Said an angry old farmer of Barnes
B'aint no sense 'avin barns witout varms
    All this glass architecture's
    A stoopid old gesture
Can' eat glass, them town types never larns.

A gourmet of East Waterloo
Rejected a dish of tofu
    Saying ostrich is nice
    But I'd rather have mice
Or a snail saucied out with a tutu.

An obscurantist painter of Blackwall
Splashed two dots of black on a white wall
    Then expounded his thesis
    Profound exegesis -
And was hailed as a genius transcending all.

EUTISM, 1990s

A poem must not rhyme or search for beauty
It must avoid all mystery, magic, duty
Reliquish every trace of neo-Gothic
All idealism, real or idiotic
Reject the rhythm of our blood, the seasons
Restrict the theme to image, pointless reasons
The best of poetry is very subtle
Obscurely meaningless, a buried truffle
It needs a pig to sniff out its location
Or swarm of flies purporting putridation.

SAINT VALENTINE

Be thou my song and I will be thy lay
Be thou my corset I will be thy stay
Be thou my love and I will be thy lover
Be thou my life and I will be thy liver

SPRING, A RESURRECTION

Spring! and we think of new born lambs
Haloed in crystal sun
Clouds softly drifting over limpid skies
Bleak winter done

Greedily stems suck up the rising sap
Swelling the buds tight-stitched in wintery scales
Veins of the fragile leaves unclasp their folds
Like infant bat's wings spreading out green sails

Under the warming earth the seeds awake
Powerful as moles they thrust through crushing clay
Gripped by one powerful aim, to reach the light
Tilt to the sun's progression round the day

Greyly the silken pussy willows gleam
Drowsy as kittens curled up tight in sleep
Lengthening yellow catkins tumble down
Tremble with gold as misty sunbeams sweep

Freshness and wonder permeate the land
Bright butterflies erupt from crysales
Tadpoles abound in ponds where willows weep
And carp flush red in blue reflected skies

Passing too quick, ephemeral as dawn
When dewy cobwebs spark their tinsel strands
Spring's fragile radiance of rain-drenched pools
Coarsens and thickens in hot summer's hands

Blossoms cascade like myriad waterfalls,
Struggle for space with brash unruly stems
Fade into fruits and seeds and falling leaves
Sink and lie prone, a passive requiem

Skeletal in the coffin of the winter's night
Beneath the frosted dish of pewter moon
With trees etched black against the ice-floed skies,
Spring waits, like Lazarus, to be renewed.

STILL WATERS SHIVER

Still waters shiver in the winds of March
Grey skies weep ice
Snow swirls from cloud-tossed skies
Hard grains of rice

The pavements pound with wild dogs' slithering claws
Their bony paws
Hurl against jean-tight crotch, their slavering jaws
Maul faces raw

Each breath becomes a swallowed sword of pain
Gasped from the gale
Splinters of freezing rain snatch at the heat
My lips exhale

I rush inside and push the door shut tight
Let the wind roar
Shriek from the rooftops, pummel shuttered panes
In warmth I thaw

But quivering snowdrops blasted in the frost
Hang their pale heads
While furry insects hide themselves in sleep
Flowers' seeds are dead.

THE OTHER SIDE OF VIOLET

Violet of thunderous clouds and darkening skies
Lining the thin-split indigo of rainbow's arch
Spanning green fields where clustered drops of rain
Splinter in jewels the sparkling sunshine rays

Violet, a modest velvet-petalled flower
Scent of the herb-wild hills of warm Provence
Crystallised sweet of ice-topped fairy cakes
Allied to royal purple, sap of crushed sea snails
Deeper than leaf-juice woad and indigo
Colour of coal-tar dyes, and amethyst . . .
Take one step on, just past the violet's rim,
And fall into an unseen spirit world
Of coldly spectral *ultra*-violet waves
Unearthly mystic scene where phosphors glow
Eroded writings light up palimpsests
And honey bees and birds can feel at home.

Angel and devil, shafting from the sun
Magically changing oxygen to form ozone
That wraps the world in pale blue-tinted cloud
Guarding our flesh from lethal outer rays,

Maker of life itself when earth new-born
Was swirled about by vaporous methane
Their chaos UV-stilled to DNA
Genetic code, amino-acid chain

Menacing, vital, god of love and wrath
You could not let your good creation rest
A mutagen, a dread carcinogen,
You goaded cells to suicidal death,
Wanton, destroyed, to be more manifest.

ENWOMBED

I felt a thudding rhythm that
Pulsated through my blood
I heard gut-thunder rumbling though
My ears were only buds
I was cosy fed and watered, floating
Darkly in my space
An encapsulated aeronaut
Placenta'd to my base

Of smell of taste of sound of sight
Perception left me free
But proprioceptors in my heart
And muscles guided me
I knew no anger, fear or hate
While I was in the womb
No envy, jealousy or greed
No presaging of doom

Yet I was truly active, all
Systems fortified
Building hormones, enzymes, nerves and bones
To fight my way outside

Oh blinding light, appalling sound,
Cruel drag of gravity
Gross input, isolation, dread,
Set out to shatter me

Fond lovers in their warm embrace
Find Paradise regained
Enchantment, unity and trust
Umbilically enchained

But how can I recapture
That preternatural state?
With knees drawn up against my chin
I try to meditate

Slough off this clay which binds me
Like a limpet to a buoy,
Leap lightly as a rush of wind
Insensate save for joy
Let my body lie abandoned in
The cold damp fungal earth
With narcissistic ecstasy
I'll nullify my birth

FOOTSTEPS SOUND ON THE STAIR

Footsteps sound on the stair - there's no one there
Shadows loom on the wall
Across the empty hall

Out of the horrors of a demented mind
Smash whine and grind
Grey shadows waver though there's no known source
Doors that are locked swing open without force

Arrows of terror pierce the very soul
Turning the eyes to coal
The brain to ice
Clamped in a vice

My limbs are heavy, blood is vampire-drained
A crushing sea of fear holds me enchained
My thudding heart shakes till my ribs convulse
Strained ears are deafened by my thundering pulse . .

There's nothing there? Then what's reality?
If others see not that which I can see
Is what I see a mere futility
When what is real to them is lost on me?
No, they must doubt that they are real to me.

DEATH

I heard a voice as clear as murmuring streams
That filled the room with music of the spheres
A mist embraced me, cool and moisture-sweet
Soft touch of snowflakes melting on my skin
Time fell away as in a lift ascending
And in the twilight of desire our bodies blended
He sang me poems that were thin as gruel
Yet pierced with radiance, enchanted tales
Of childhood, love, regrets, of faith and fears.

My body insubstantial, real as shade
Melted and drifted as time decomposed
Fading to thinness, now invisible
Now permeating walls, the very trees
The air, the sky, the people I had known
Waking or sleeping, sentient or dead
Bonded together, magnet-like, suffused

I thought I stood above a waterfall,
I thought the sky poured dreams
My atoms sprang apart, bright airborne spray
My body lightened as the earth grew dim
Ghosts drifted shadow-dark beneath the trees
Floating suspended, forms that gently writhed
And coalesced and parted, mists windblown
Through fluid worlds of underwater seas

Where all was one in space, in time, in feeling,
In life, in death,
And death
Was utter freedom.

COUNTRY LIVING
(PLUS ÇA CHANGE)

The cottage walls were made of stone,
Above the slanting eves
The rosy tiles were scalloped, speckled
Starlings perched and gleamed.

An ancient couple lived there, both
Withdrawn into the past
Their sight and hearing fading, from
The world around outcast.
All day he mumbled, muttered through
Dryly parted lips -
As regrets rose up like acid burps
A windy curse outripped.

An extrovert colossus, she
Was quite without restraint
Her voice was as abrasive as
A varnish-stripping paint.
She was insanely greedy, her
Obsessive fingers crammed
Black pudding, faggots, savaloys
Between her yellowed fangs.

The bedroom floor shook as they walked
A wall clock loudly ticked
The iron-framed beds had patchwork quilts
And mattresses like bricks.
Religious oleographs stared down
In glossy garish hues
On candlesticks and chamber pots
Rush matting, light diffused.

She sat there in a wicker chair
That creaked as if in pain
And peered between the curtains through
The diamond-leaded pane.

Her shallow forehead furrowed,
Steel-rimmed glasses on her nose
She sighed and dreamed of lovers as
She read romantic prose
As if it nourished part of her
That food could never calm
Her torment for the might-have-beens
Successfully embalmed.

He had a secret sorrow, long
Engraved upon his heart -
His first wife's name he'll murmur as
His soul and body part.

- . - . - . -

Their grandchildren saw neither the
Grotesqueness nor the tears
They accepted without question what
Was real was what appeared.
They gloried in the mystery of
Wooding through the trees
Or up steep hills to copses ripe
With sun-warmed blackberries.

The heady smell of boiling jam
Of baking, thrilled their souls
Bread puddings stuffed with raisins, spicy
Buns and sausage rolls.
They toasted bread on long-armed forks
Before the embers red
And played at snakes and ladders till
She sent them off to bed.

A soot-encrusted kettle always
Simmered on the hob
The milky tea distilled wood smoke -
Ambrosia for the gods!
The creepy spider corners, crackling
Fires that shot out sparks,
The wasps that drowned in jamjar traps
Owls hooting in the dark,
The clash of bells upon the air
On quiet summer eves
That harmonised with cows' and sheep's
Divine cacophonies . . .

_ · _ · _ · _

The old folks now are buried, he
Imprisoned by her weight
Crushed in the grave to silence
Till they disintegrate.

It's a far cry from suburbia
Pine panelling and woks
From vegan fare and microwaves
Hand-woven rugs and smocks.
Instead of country dialects
Soft as the drone of bees
New Sloane-clone accents rend the air
Sharp as a winter's breeze.

The nouveaux riches arrive in droves
- It has to be the trend -
They've bought up all the cottages
That used to be condemned.
They think it's great to rusticate
In welly boots and jeans
The footpaths have been privatised
The pub is haute cuisine.

No longer are the gardens full
Of dahlias, hollyhocks,
Bright daisies and the glorious smell
Of evening-scented stocks,
Of onions, sprouts and carrots
In regimented rows
Long runner beans with scarlet flowers
Potatoes freshly hoed.

The almond-perfumed wallflowers
The golden gooseberries
Have given way to brasher tints
Of cobalt and cerise.
An artificial life for sure
These youthful philistines
With their videos, camcorders, pigeon
Shooting, riding, vines.

Does the hard and glossy cellulose
The polished nagahyde
Conceal synthetic stuffing, or
Is something real inside?
Has currency replaced their thoughts
And grappling hooks their hearts
Or is the rat-race syndrome just
A shield against life's darts?

Their defence is more successful since
It rests on crass display
Cars, houses, lands, boats, cottages -
We must have more than they.
They'd never recognise their link
With that impoverished pair
But we all need some safe refuge from
The ragings of despair.

My dreams are strangers stalking through the night
Ephemera beyond the scrim of real
Identities obscured in mist's evasive swirl.
They lay a treasure-trail of Easter eggs
Encoding clues and cryptic messages
That waver, fading as I bend to read
Air-brushed away by memories loss-lorn.

Then startlingly the background lightens dim to bold
A spotlight brilliance focussed sharp, no shade:
A small and lively dog runs quickly in
His claws a light click-clack upon the floor
He gulps the food placed in his dinner bowl
Contented, licks his jaws -

Then pauses, swivels head in shocked dismay
As strange new puppy lollops in, all bounce and fun
Welcomed with giggles, hugs and slobbery tongue.
They do not see the small dog slink away
With sideways glances crouching low to hide,
His anguished eyes sick with a jealous pain
Under their fringe of hair
Appear to cry.

Smooth the scene changes, without hitch or pause
Devoid of logic, lacking causal sequence
The tiny dog's transformed into a girl
Just three years old
Leaning against her mother's chair
Her sultry eyes
Peering beneath a fringe of hair
Glower at the lively puppy now a new-born brother
Sucking at the breast
But weakly, falling often into sleep
The nipple slipping slackly from his lips
His soft breath drifting, petals from a flower.

The mother's heart congeals with grief and fear
The little girl, wanting to hug her, wants to hit her too
Her love and hate inseparably blended
As when a fluid shimmering shifting light
Racing across shot silk
Floods it with green then purple
Green again, sliding together
Back and forth,
Moment by moment.

She loves her brother, tiny, pale and beautiful
His silk-soft wisps of reddish-golden hair
His every movement, every feature magical
She wants him to be hers and hers alone
She wants her mother for herself alone
But now in rage, desolate, feeling unwanted
Underloved, excluded and neglected
She wants him dead.

Slow the stage darkens as the image fades -
Then from the dimness shoots a beam of light
Homed on a coffin silent, white
A nest of swansdown holds a waxen doll.
In quietness, hushed, the whispering curtains fall
Black as a pall.

Prologue

It's summer at a boarding house, north Cornwall.
Beyond the panes of glass the sand and sea
Stretch to infinity.
Sitting around a table in the sun
A man and woman and their two small children

The boy is four, his hair a blonde-white cloud,
His eyes sky-blue.
The girl is two,
Bronze eyes and copper hair, cut square,
Staring intently as if she could bore
Straight through the surface
To an inner core.

The landlady, broad spoken, settles down the tray

Nods at the mother's convex-swollen belly
Another one?
And while the mother smiles
The girl in fury glowers at both of them
Enraged to have been kept in ignorance
Yet strangers told!

Seeing her scowling face the woman offers, cosy,
Thinking to make her feel important
I expect you'd like your milk in a glass?
No! she says clearly, voice a fledgling piping,
Glass is for babies!.
They laugh,
She smoulders.

Epilogue

The baby's buried, grave encased in snow.
The mother's breast
Full now to bursting with unneeded milk
Seeking to ease the agonising ache
Offers the little girl who cannot sleep
Her nipple's consolation
But the child, alarmed,
Pushes her hard away
It's not her milk!
Caught in the tightness of a personal pain
Each turns away, bearing her grief alone.

And dangling from the walls, long crinkly brown,
Hang the dry toast-crisp fronds of bladderwrack
Still clung with grains of sand
Ripe ocean smells
Momento of the rocks and crab-lurked pools
Of seaside holiday
Six months ago.

TIMELESS

I walk one April evening in the garden
The sky's awash with opalescent blue
The silver birch tree fans its lacy branches
Its tender leaflets strung, green drops of dew.

Hen pheasants nestle in the warmth of fern fronds
Straggling their rough brown arms down dry-stone walls,
The grass is strewn with ghost-pale primrose clusters
The silence hung with birds' clear rippling calls.

The moon dull white, its crumbly flesh half-eaten,
Grows brighter as the glow of sunset fades
Plump rabbits skitter over dew-damp grasses
Scuts fluorescent as the dark invades.

Time's spell hangs softly on the hush of evening
A flock of pigeons clatter into flight
Exploding from the ash tree's topmost branches -
And wild-life whiskers pause to check the night.

Cool, in the dusk, a breath of air blows softly
Stirring the ashes of the smouldering fire
Into a blaze where witches' eyes in caverns
Glare out in hatred from their torturing pyre.

As time stands still, the atmosphere regresses
Hooves muffled by a rug of fallen leaves
Out from the trees King Arthur's horse comes clopping
penants flying
His knights dull-bright in helmet, breast and greaves.

They're gone. As pouncing owls hoot out a warning
Green shadows glide around the wood's dark glades
Bow twangs and swishing arrow finds its target
The deer outrun exhausted falls, legs splayed.

A huntsman's horn a pack of hounds soft baying
A fox that races past straight tail a-stream
A poacher hung around with gins and snare-wires
A crying child, a lover's hungering dream.

The centuries unfold their layered hindsight
In footsteps, lingering glances, aching tears
Each act repeated, shifting, fading, merging
Dropped like thin ghosts in graves of echoing years.

I raise my eyes and on the far horizon
Town lights' synthetic pink blots out the stars
The distant drone of traffic carries faintly
An aircraft's silhouette, a pulse that jars.

I turn to face the present and its problems
The wavering window panes reflect the moon
Within there's rush light, flickering candle, oil lamp smoking
Bent heads, sore eyes, old shadows haunt the room.

Against the ancient chimney, rising cloudwards
The TV aerial perches, one-legged stork
The earth moves on, each moment passed for ever
Each dying day ephemeral as thought.

AUNT VIOLET

She nearly wrecked my life, Aunt Violet
Now decades later memory makes me sweat.
When younger she had been a bold coquette
A fierce and rabble-rousing martinet
Chained to the railings like a Suffragette.
And then she married George, a baronet
Who sadly died, drowned in a rivulet.
Her stately home was down in Somerset
Stone windows clustered round with pale rosettes
In floral borders fragrant mignonette -
She loved to tuck the sprigs, like amulets,
Within her bodice lining's sarcenet.
She taught me all the rules of etiquette
Some words I must not say, like serviette.
Dark evenings in her bogus coronet
She'd act out some quite naughty novelette
Supporting roles by Sam the Paroquette
And stunts by Acrobatic Marmoset.
Sometimes again we'd dance a minuet
Strictly to tempo like a marionette
With live musicians playing a quartet.
At other times, her tortoiseshell lorgnette
Poised on her nose, she'd read *The Times* gazette
Or play some games around the alphabet
Compete to write the funniest sestet,
Nibbling the holder of her cigarette.
Alas she was addicted to roulette
Lost all her money, then without regret
She jumped one night from off the parapet
And left me all her debts
So I should not forget, *dear* Violet.

MOTHER LOVE

The mother salamander pops her eggs upon her head
And carries them a towering yellow hat,
For snakes and shrews are eyeing them to feed their young instead
And she must risk her life if they attack.

The terrifying alligator's huge and thorny jaws
Could snap a man in half, yet when she hears
The tiny bird-like chirruping of newly hatching young
Her mother's tenderness in full appears

She waddles to their burial place and digs into the ground
While humming a contralto counterpoint
The wriggly swarming youngsters clamber up into her mouth
And riverwards she shuttles to anoint.

The elephant seems clumsy and of monumental size
Her calf when born drops four feet to the mud
But when it stands she nuzzles it and loops her trunk around
Its shoulders in a warm and friendly hug.

The dolphin stands no nonsense, if her infant starts to tease
She holds it firmly to the ocean base
Until it's very nearly drowned and then she takes its flipper
And they waggle up to reach the water surface.

The cat although domestic and perhaps at times confused
Resorts to corporal punishment if need be
She will growl and slap her kitten's face then lick it hard all over
To show if it obeys there's no hard feeling.

The sacred Bali monkey which is known as the macaque
Will grab her baby's tail to stop it straying . . .
And so on through the Kingdom high and low, and big and small
It's mother love that stops the race decaying.

But when we come to humans they have lost the basic skill
Of knowing just exactly what to do
The well of instinct though not dry is buried in tradition
And overlaid with fashion and taboo

We think too much, are bludgeoned by the blows of mixed advice
Let medicine take the strains of death or life
We talk instead of showing, and we shop not hunt for food,
We punish but omit the reassurance.

While other babies imitate their parents' natural functions
For humans artificial is the key
There's cars and telly, mobile phones, a status house and garden
So sod the mother love, we want more money.

THE FLEETING HOURS

The fleeting hours grow shorter every day
Wafting my life away
My thoughts like writhing snakes twine me with spells
My ageing flesh repels

Long-past regrets as frightened deer upstart
Rending my heart apart
The decades pass before me incomplete
Mocking my life effete

All day I sit and watch the film reel roll
Flirting with lives I stole
The envied young are angels cast in gold
Dreaming a life untold

Their silken skin, their limbs, their freefall gait
Grieving I contemplate
I see them snatch the happiness I missed
Basking in being kissed

But when they too are old they'll sit as I
Singing a swan's last cry
Their endless hourless days inconsequent
Struggling to seem content

Yet surely it was I indulged those ploys
Failing to count the joys
Engorged with zest that made the senses swim
Pitying falls from sin

Oh such is life - each touch each sweet caress
Fosters our greediness
Each sumptuous meal augments our hunger-pain
Yearning to eat again

Each love magnetic, soaring with delight
Freshens the appetite
We long for night, we crave return of day
Gambling time's roundelay

The leaves burst forth, are dropped, burst forth again
Rambling through memory's pain
Our seasons lead us only towards the slope
Dreading the loss of hope

My life descending seeks to climb once more
Fleeing from Lethe's shore
I stretch my arms, a would-be conqueror
Pleading with deaf-eared Fate *Encore! Encore!*

WITCHCRAFT

Moonlight, starlight, incantations,
Dying cows and sickly hens
Brain distempers, gut disorders
Deadly curses strike men down
Skin black-crusted, visions shifting
Mega-spiders creeping wild
Children blind or wasting slowly
Lethargy that frays the mind
Stunted limbs and bloodied sputum
Spuds that rot within the ground
Plague of locusts, drought perpetual
Earthquakes floods and thunder sounds
Crocodiles become bisexual
Sheep miscarry, dogs go mad
Pestilence, the Black Death pustules,
Spreading through congested land. . .

In the Middle Ages man was
Ruled by ignorance and dread
All disasters dark with horror
God of wrath might strike him dead
Terrified he saw his failings
Sweating panic, trembling sighs -
Three old crones passed cackling toothless
Giving him the evil eye!
Suddenly he saw salvation
Wickedness externalised
Surrogates for his damnation
Cursed evil, Satan's brides
Racks will make them see their malice
At the stake they'll rise in flames
In their pain they'll find purgation
Free him from their hideous games . . .

Now that science knows the causes
BSE and CJD
Prions poisoning the nerve cells
Salmonella romping free
Ultra-violet multiplying
Harmful cells beneath the skin
LSD hallucinations
Drugs not spells pollute within
Radio-active earth and pastures
Red blood cells are crucified
Nuclear fall-out, tranquilisers
Gene mutations, pesticides
Clogged up lungs from dust asbestos
In the soil spores multiply
Waves from sun's magnetic pulses
Rabid dogs, and ergot rye
Hormone substitutes in water
Giving males a female thrust
Insect populations peaking
Vector-fleas and lice and bugs. . .

Science knows both cause and answers
Keeps its secrets, will not tell
Truths obscured by politicians
Knowledge is their source of power
Burn the cows and burn the chickens
Kill the germs that cause disease
Better still the politicians
Pledged to votes and moneyed ease
They would have us like the peasants
Back in superstition's thrall
Live in fear dependent on their
Wicked failure to inform.

WORDS

Words can have music like a violin
Can bounce with rhythm like a trampolene
Can roar and rattle like a big base drum
Clash like brass cymbals, whisper harmonies
Move us to laughter, tears, despair and anger
Horror or wonder, reverence or fear

Yet words are only letters on a page
Assembled in a predetermined order
The letters in themselves devoid of meaning
Like notes of music, trails of dots and tails
Climbing and falling up and down a scale
Until translated, music into sound
The glorious vibrancy of shaking air
As ear drums quiver to the rippling waves

Such arbitrary marks are art's raw symbols
The paints and brushes, chisels, potter's wheel
An artifice of man, remote from nature
Where squirrels chattering, songs of nightingales
The piping shrill of dolphins in the sea
Are language without words or thought or reason
Unconscious made, unconscious recognition.

But words when put together out of letters,
Juggled and ordered into sentences
Manipulated into argument,
Make tales and discourse, politics and ploys,
Abstruse philosophies of Schopenhauer and Freud

Of all the forms of art it's words alone
That never lose their link with reasoning brain
The other arts aim at our raw emotion
And falling short no words will ever save them
Failed art is art that lacks communication

But poetry! the peak of verbal art
Combining sound with sense, shrewdness with feeling
A perfect blending of the heart and mind
Words to be savoured, dwelt upon, carressed
Their melodies entwined, or shot like arrows
Their consonants and vowels, their rhyme and rhythm
Their volume, cadence, phrasing, repetition
Their variations on a theme - a song unsung
Just letters, but they need no other music.

VARMINTS

How sweet the rabbits deer and other vermin
White-tufted scuts, dark eyes with softness yearning
As they consume the roses, nibble bark
Eat all the flowers and leave the gardens stark

Keen foxes dig the earth and moles raise mountains
While vixen burn the grass with urine
And deer top freshly planted trees
And tits devour the buds and seeds
And blackbirds, starlings spoil the fruit
And squirrels tear the lead from roofs
Slip into attics find a hoard -
Stored apples chase across the board
Like eerie poltergeists at bowls -
Mark each with teeth to claim the whole
And foxes gaily kill for fun
Flamingos, hens and geese - a ton
And bees in walls can bring disaster
As honey seeps down through the plaster
While fur-farm escapees the mink
Drive fishermen to madness' brink . . .

So sad to kill! and yet we must
Or they would rule the world not us.

They have no money, no religion
No Stock Exchange, no Inquisition
We poison rivers, overfish,
Catch unseen waves within a dish
Wear holes in earth's protective screen
Desex ourselves with oestrogen
Defoliate the shrubs and trees
Sole source of nutrient energies
Make lethal weapons, nuclear rays
And change the weather - if it pays
Then, all for God, evict the heathen
Shoot him, starve him, till he's beaten
We are obliged to save his soul
Besides his land is full of gold.

The thought-less beasts are powered by race-fruition
But sapient Man knows best, his race: ambition
Survival-instinct long since in attrition
So wise, he'll kill himself with narcissism.

THE ROOM GROWS COLD

The room grows cold,
Beneath the curtained door
An icy draft writhes like a snake
Across the floor
Coils round my ankles
By conduction steals my heat.

The air refrigerating
Gathers weight,
Stiffens my limbs to rigor
As my frozen eyes
Catch,
In the darkest corner of the room,
A gliding shape no more than aery mist
Drifting towards me, hesitant and weak.

It emanates a deep-freeze chill
Laying itself like frozen packages along my skin
Burning with frost
Sucking the vital heat
Out of my body in a vaporous sweat
That builds the image up
Giving it substance
Shape more firm
My energy converted into matter -
As they say one day computers will
Solely from energy
Make solid food.

It's coming nearer
Gaining form and colour
Draining the heat of firelight
So that it flickers
Leaping flames shrink back
Wood dulls and blackens
Smoulders and goes out.

Now fortified, the tissue paper flatness
Swells to a third dimension
Leaning towards me, mocking
Face malevolent
Noting my falling body heat, my shallow breath
Metabolism hijacked by this ghost.

My heart beats slow, on hold
A threatening hand
Grabs up a vase and throws it
Smash against a wall.
Faintly I hear a laugh
Like a hen's cackling triumph
As it lays an egg.

And suddenly the room is black as coal
The lights have failed
Only a wavering luminescence left
Gaining insidiously in size and strength
In malice and in power -
It's commandeered the main's electric voltage
For its own selfish purposes!

This common burglar, this monstrosity,
Energy-grabber, vandal!
Hacking the power supply that I must pay for
Just to materialise at my expense.
What are you, infiltrator?
Some creature from the past? the present? future?
Mars? A distant solar system?
Spatial fourth dimension?

You anger me,
Shadowy likeness, simulacrum, virtual real!
You want my body?
Right, I'll swap with you
But you're a fool
Have you forgotten what it's like
To be enclosed in flesh
No more than tick-tock engine to a lump of clay?

You're really growing fat
Don't fool yourself, don't for a moment think
Once you are me
You'll ever pass through solid walls again
Electro-magnetism will repulse your matter
You'll never see again in people's minds
Or breathe your icy breath upon their feelings
Making their hairs prick up, their skins goosepimple
And if it's cruelty that really turns you on
Let me remind you
Intimidation is a criminal offence.

Never again you'll pass unseen
Vanishing, rematerialising,
In other houses, countries, galaxies.
Like any human you'll be tied to earth's space-time
Stranger to certainty
Restricted to this world of
Speculation, guesswork, probability . . .

Why should I warn you?
Come on, in you get,
I'm longing to escape
Here, take my feelings, worries, illnesses
My pains, my obligations, all the chores,
Swaddle yourself in this embodiment of flesh
Restrained by muscle, bone and joint formation
By lifespan limitations -
I'm away!

The being pauses, stares, turns pale and faint
I feel a warmth soften my frozen limbs
The wood glows red, the flames begin to dance
The lights come on
The ghost, now vague and two-dimensional,
Recedes
Drifts through the wall,
Not looking back,
Is gone.

AIRBORNE ON SPRINGS

I wish I were aerial
Because I'd like to fly
Not in a jumbo liner
Miles up into the sky
But with my own ethereal wings,
airborne on springs

I'd like to skim the rooftops
And spy through windows bare
Not exactly voyeurism
Just to see who's what and where
How other people live their lives,
secret in hives

The distant constellations
Circumnavigate the globe
But there's nothing in the zodiac
That outer space can probe
No bird or bat or flying-cat,
or even gnat

I know there can be scorpions
And shaggy long-horned bulls
While Aquarians carry water
To fill the dried-up pools
And mollify the fish and crabs,
and spotted dabs

The archers have their arrows
And the libras have their scales
To shoot the other symbols
Or to weigh the watery pails
But they will never help me zoom,
nearer the moon

Some people can be leos
Or curly-headed rams
Or randy goats that leap about
And pinch each other's hams -
And still the stars perambulate,
sealing my fate

The rest is rather nonsense
For how can one be twins
Both separate and together
Like innocence and sins -
Yet virgos clutter up the lands,
with crowded prams

But when I am an angel
With wings that cannot melt
My own celestial body
And a zodiacal belt
I'll soar above the counterscarp,
strumming my harp.

AUTUMN, A CHANCE TO SLEEP

The dew sets sparkling diamonds in the grass
Made green and purple by the slanting rays
That glance from sinking sun through wisps of mist
Floating above the puddles left by rain

Gone are the agonies of spring, the scorching sun
The frantic thrust of stems hell-bent to gain
The light and air, preserve their pedigrees
Proffering their hearts to passing bumblebees

This end achieved their choking growth can cease
Fulfilled, the plants sink back towards the earth
Like business men relaxing at their clubs
Complacently reviewing what they've won

Redundant leaves tumble in tipsy sway
Pert children seeking to prolong their play
Cushions of moss like emerald velveteen
Toadstools displayed in pallid tangerine

Then desiccated leaves, dry mummied mice
Scrabble their scratchy claws across the path
Racing at speed before the errant wind
Tossing wild hair into the empty air

The frogs are burrowing down beneath the mud
The fish now sluggish drowse between the reeds
The restless squirrels store away their stacks
Of future oak trees for their winter snacks

The wind, the rain, the low hung harvest moon
Clear frosty skies, domed blackness pierced with stars
Leaf colours fiery as the setting sun
Then brown, drab green, the year is nearly done

The smoke of bonfires fills the balmy air
We rake up all the trash of yesteryear
Outdated as the news we threw away . .

The naked trees look down on dull brown earth
Seeming to sway in grief
Moaning their twigs to peace
But what they softly sigh's a lullaby
Glad the long days are ended
Glad that the dark will give them
A chance to sleep.

LADIES WITH CELLOS

Ladies with cellos sitting in the dusk
Sweet-talking nightingales to air their voice
On summer evenings when the woods are still
When leaves hang silent,
Hushed and warm the air,
Gently the cellos' bows
Carress the strings
Filling the night with rich and vibrant sound
Luringly drifting through the spellbound trees
Wooing the birds like sirens in the sea

Till suddenly pours through the starry dark
A silver waterfall of song
Weaving through cello notes a liquid thread
Cascading from the sky
Clear as a mountain stream
Cadence of pure delight
Undying passion . . .

Nothing but darkness, music and entrancing song

Is this an avian Cyrano hiding his tenderness
Concealed within the blackness of the night?
Or rather an enchanted conjurer
Plundering his magic repertoire of song
Plucking as from a crowded box of jewels
Bright gems of sound
Dazzling the air with diamonds, rubies,
Emeralds, pearls
Enticing onwards, star-struck, hypnotised
Some blind-date hen to be his season's bride?

Imagination robes him in majestic garb
Gives him the stature of a deity
Inspiring relic from those bygone days
Of towering Romeos and awesome knights
When legendary figures walked the earth
And there was dignity nobility
A world of time eternal, love immortal
Beauty entrancing, feelings pure and true
A world of infancy bereft of guile
Direct, undoubting.

Only at evening time his glorious voice
Sweetly seductive as the pipes of Pan
Or lyre of Orpheus that charmed the stones -
Trills with melodious passion
By day immersed in practicalities
His song transformed to clarion call of challenge
He hunts for insects, guards his hen and young -
Night song discarded for domestic toils

So summer passes, fledgelings leave the nest
Triggered by instincts anciently inborn
Drawn by the magnet of the winter sun
His small brown insignificance lifts from the tree
Wings beating on, four thousand monstrous miles
Across the mountains, seas, Saharan sands . .

A hurricane of sadness marks his wake
Pale memories haunt the woods in eddying wraiths
Dull days are fractured by banality
Life lacks enhancement, smouldering ashes fade . . .

Then April's back. As quiet of twilight falls
The nightingale expands his heart anew
Freshness and wonder, peace and calm content,
Carress the night with lilting billet-doux.

FISHING FOR TIDDLERS

Blue, green and gold
Sky, grass and buttercups
Varnished in glinting light
Colours of sunny childhood
On the whiskered bank
Cluttered with cuckoo flowers
Where the stream flows
Under the hump-backed bridge,
Eddies of liquid glass
Round the dark stones
Powdered with loose grey algae
Time-neglected dust.

Here, in the shallows, tiddlers silver-backed
Flash through the dimness
Shadowed by our heads,
Bent closely gazing.

So I now gaze
Into the waters of my memory
Where remote,
Safe in another place another time,
The fishes of my childhood wink at me
Swimming and gliding
Brilliant waves of light
Rippling in shoals
Clear topaz eyes
Fixed in their shining circles,
Tiny puppet mouths
Opening and closing
Speaking in silence.

We lowered jamjars
Necks entwined with string
So they lay open-ended
Tempting fish to enter -
Then impatient
Dragged the jar fast along the gravel
Swooping, a whale's horrific jaws,
Into the darting swarms
Scraping the algal spores
That rose in lazy clouds
Muddying crystal water.

Small hands held up the haul
Marvelled at bodies
Circling so rapidly around and round
OD'd on joy -
Or was it panic?
We gave them grass to eat and
Stood them in the sun
Knowing so knowledgeably
They needed warmth and food
To stay alive.

Yet one by one
Their undulating bodies - thrashing, lunging,
Heads arched back
Their thin mouths overstretched -
Turned stiff and still and belly-up
Expired.

Like watery minnows,
Far-off memories
Gleam in the shallows of my childhood's dreams
Elusive as the breath of fairy tales
Where ghosts and witches
Elves and goblins, giants
Lure my gaze inwards, downwards
Tranced by their mystery
Swift as bright arrows
Streaks of molten silver
Gliding and turning
Till my mind
Suddenly triggered by a distant image
Faint with time
Dips in to snatch it upwards
Cupped in my hollowed hand
Aching to know
Re-know
The secrets of my lifetime's past
Adsorb its haunting to reality.

Poor isolated wretch of memory
Wrenched from the cool of water
Daylight-screened,
Choked in the rising heat of human skin
It strains with filmy fins
To thrust against the unresisting gas,
Lashing its iridescent tail
And wildly gulping air it cannot use.
All its emotive haunting
Once so strong
Drains from its turned-dull scales
Till it lies rigid
Drab and dead,
Still there
But with its life quite gone.

'THE BLISS OF SOLITUDE'
(WORDSWORTH)

The clouds are oil paint ridges
Stormy grey and white
Riding the canvas of the silent sky.
Beside the road tall trunks of conifers
Recede into deep woods, shrinking away
Into the dark of space and into time
Their swooping branch tips slyly watching
The passer-by.
In tufted fields the grass
Sprouts in coarse sun-bleached tussocks
Highlit hair
The posts of dried-out wood
Dark-crusted with a lichen's curly beard
Hold tight-stretched wires
Ragged with shards of wool
Scattered like shredded paper
Over the bleak ground
Here sheep stand still as wooden toys
Their meat-thick bodies perched
On bone-thin legs
Their shabby wool clotted with leaves and oil
Each lower jaw locked into ruminating mode
Their glass-fixed eyes
Glaring resentfully
Out of a mask of balaclava black
While near them hover lambs hoof-poised
To run to mother
Butt her with bone-hard heads
Pummeling her pendulous milk sacs like a punching bag
Mouths turning up to suck
Tails wagging wildly in anticipation.
She walks away from them, straddles her legs and pees
Beside the tiny stream
Clinking its glinting mini-waterfalls
Scattering the light
Around the worn-smooth stones
The clumps of rushes
Harsh with the smell of dung.

Beside the loch a willow droops
Its long straight hair.
Smooth in the wind's absence
The water slaps the shore
In languid pulses
Where the reeds poke up
And liver-spotted cows
Feed leisurely
While in the air the high
Soprano voices of castrated lambs
Blend with the eerie cries of seagulls swooping
Beyond the hedge where blackened pods of broom
Cling like dried scabs of blood
To withered branches.

Small and far away
A solitary walker now appears
Where the road bends
And the high voltage pylons thrust across the hills
Scored with a dozen shades of green and gold
And rape, bright yellow.
He eyes the landscape
In the wild distance
Wary as flat-skulled sheep
Innately disinclined to trust a stranger
Could-be danger.